Explaining Everything

Poems by Bruce Horovitz

Cleveland State University Poetry Center
Cleveland Poets Series No. 37

ACKNOWLEDGMENTS

Grateful acknowledgment is made to the publications listed below, in which some of these poems first appeared.

"Waving at Planes Over Dayton" appeared in *Diddean,* Carmel Pine Cone Press, 1979.

"Like the Year Richie Scheinbloom Went O for 64" appeared in *Pig Iron Baseball,* Pig Iron Press, Youngstown, 1982.

"The Poker Chips in My Grandmother's Closet" appeared in *Berkeley Poetry Review,* University of California Press, Berkeley, 1976.

Cover art by Terril Neely.

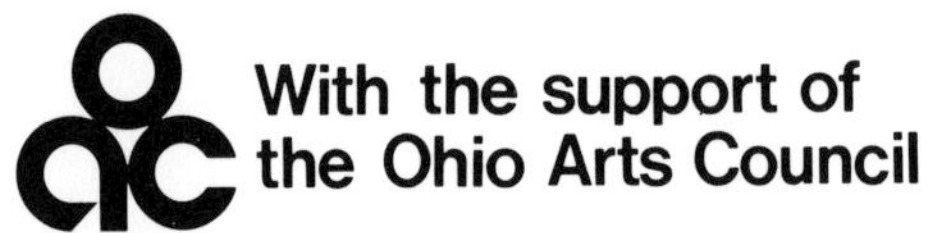

ISBN 0-914946-46-3

For Mom and Dad

A POEM THAT WILL BEGIN
JUST AS SOON AS EVERYONE GETS HERE

Where is that 300 pound French woman
who practically made me invite her?
And where is her friend, or sister,
the one who lunches on white chocolate?
What about the guy from Redhook, New Jersey
who sells automobile seat covers?
How can I begin without him?
Where are the yogurt eaters?
My neighbors who keep telling me
it is yummy and healthy and cheap.
Do me a favor. Find the guy
who works the car wash and forgot
to put down my antenna.
I tell you, he's supposed to show.
What happened to the old lady
upstairs who sits with her heat turned off?
Where is she?
Can you find the eye, ear, and throat
doctor who told me I have to specialize?
Has anyone seen the produce clerk
who knows a good zucchini when he feels one?
Where are the hunters?
Catchem. Killem. Eatem.

Where are the people who'd spill coffee
on this poem?

LIKE THE YEAR RICHIE SCHEINBLOOM WENT 0 FOR 64

Our back porch is dryer than a pitcher's mound in What Cheer,
Iowa, where life is a stretch between innings. The men
who made this porch didn't know we'd sit out here; days,
nights, rot the steps so wood fell in like old bleachers.
This railing is a sidearmed southpaw — says it's been around.
Maybe has three more good years. It wheezes like a call
from centerfield. The wood has been leaned on.
Elbows have rubbed away any trace of grain. Our house:
a winter dugout. Everyone who's live here's been traded.

I.

WAVING AT PLANES OVER DAYTON

He tips his wing so that only part of it shows
and the sliver I can see is like the thin bottom
of a melon sitting in a field, or the moon
one night after it is full.
That pilot is thinking of me
and I am glad.
In a few hours the colors will gloat
on his instrument panel and face
and those same wings will flare red at the ends.
He will remember me all the way
to Cincinnati.

II.

WAVING DOWN AT A YOUNG BOY IN DAYTON

When I passed here, one week yesterday, that same boy
was waving. Passengers (only 8 that day) didn't know
the difference between a tipped wing and a slight change
in direction. I tell you, I saw his smile
like a boy spitting melon seeds,
or maybe like when the moon sections between two halves
of the horizon. His arms never once touched his sides.

WE COME UPON THE SPECIAL
OLYMPICS AT OHIO STATE STADIUM

i.
From a distance it looked
like a fair.
Balloons and banners.
Ronald McDonald handing out cookies
except
this time his smile is real.
The running track circles
to the man on the ladder
who starts each race by gun.
He is the most important man
in the world.

ii.
Six boys wait to be surprised.
Lane by lane
their eyes
roll easter basket smiles.
We don't know what to call them.
They all look like Charles Darling did.
Charles sat next to me in 3rd grade
and never answered questions.
They said his mother fell
down the stairs
six weeks before he was born.

iii.
Outside the stadium,
there is more.
Small activity tents.
Inside one labeled "Rock 'n Roll"
a couple makes small circles.
It is hard to see them touch.

We don't know
what to make of their
doing what we do.
Later,
we find the horseback riding ring.
Boyscouts, too young to know,
lead groups around on horses.
A girl with a tucked-in face
doesn't know
to put her feet in the stirrups.
God, she is happy.

iv.
Driving home,
a station wagon passes me
on the left.
It is filled with those same faces
I saw running and riding and laughing.
They wave, and I think
they just don't go away.
Then,
a long line of cars.
We wait hours until the source.
An overturned trailer and two dead horses.
When the station wagon rolls by
I watch all faces turn to putty.

A THANK YOU NOTE TO THE MOON

Dear Moon,

Sorry it took so long.
I guess
I got busy, or something.
I wanted to thank you
for last Friday night.
You floated big
as a highway billboard.
My room sat fat with you.
I liked after dinner
when new light made the ceiling.

Maybe we could get together again?
I'm free most evenings next week.
Except Tuesday.
That's when I take tap dance lessons.
Or maybe
you can make it for dinner.
I could bake a tuna casserole
with real tuna.
So, what do you say?
All I need is one night's
notice.

NIGHT WHISTLE

Your light is on.
Maybe you are turning night
on its side.
Or sleeping
with National Geographic;
drawing dreams
of Samoan seals.
I know the shape
of your sleep.
You have left it on my couch.
It is round as the edges
of October.
I have caught you
falling
between either side of evening.
I have watched you leave
by train.
You are the warm, night whistle
that will not hush.
I listen only
for you.

WANTING YOU ENOUGH

Every possible light
was on, your house had a door,
some windows.
I wanted you enough
to not bring back,
to find a farm in upstate New York
where blackberries explode ripe.
We would meet
our neighbors, they would borrow
from us. Come to borrow
again.

I know your eyes.
They are lights with tiny shades.
They make the points on stars.
When you look at me,
now, I am ripe for your hands.
Borrow me. Never bring me
back.

OUR WALK

Night enters our nostrils
but will not leave.
Doors on each home
sealed
like old songs.
The windows open
a little.

Look at the man
making a model.
We think,
a ship from some jigsaw puzzle.
He can make it go
inside.
Next door,
the tenured professor.
His walls calloused with dead
books.
Some have not moved
in his life.

Every house,
a picture gallery.
The black and white photo of Grandpa
when he still had
his colon.
The one of Mom
before her face fell.
Out here,
we are raw film;
no loose skin under
our necks.
That is why
we are out here.
I think,
to enjoy getting one night
older.

POWELL'S PATIO

Just past the fruit stand
on Route 20,
Powell's Patio
flashes
like a hand waving.
Powell's serves the best ice cream
this side of God.
Young girls with custard hands
work here,
turning soft, white mounds
into two-tiered lunches.
When they smile,
brake lights jam
like small planets spinning
from their axes.
Here,
sodas have middle names;
each sundae knows the secret
to the universe.
Every bite,
cool as the shady spot
where Mr. Powell plunks
his Plymouth.

THE POKER CHIPS
IN MY GRANDMOTHER'S CLOSET

My grandmother takes me
out on the roof, and says
the one good thing about living
on the seventh floor
is having Cleveland

for a backyard.
People used to socialize
up here,
and even play cards.
But now, she says, they don't

come out
at all.
Four tiny holes
squander gravel
where card table legs
dug in.

One woman thinks it is
a penthouse
and she has fenced off
a small garden
in hopes
something might grow.

My grandmother's hair
is unpinned,
because people can't see
up
seven floors.
When the wind catches it,
her hair shines like a light
left on. No one

steps out all day,
and Cleveland sits
like a deck of cards
or a garden
that hasn't been shuffled
in years.

NO ONE COULD SING IT LIKE PERRY COMO

Even Eddie Fisher knew he couldn't sing
a song like Perry Como.
A set stool raised him far above our hopes,
and Perry's white shoes never once
touched ground.
His pants had patterns that ran
with his sweaters, and the sweaters had a way
of bagging at the wrists.
Saturday night
was Perry's night.
His music filled our homes
and kept us away from the theatres.
I used to hope,
if anyone ever sent me a singing telegram,
it would be a Perry Como song.
Or better yet,
the singer would have a voice
high enough to carry a Christmas carol,
and I could pretend it was him.
Perry would hit every note,
but ran them all together
so that when he suddenly said,
"Good Night,"
we all turned off our TV sets and climbed upstairs,
to bed.

SEVERAL SENTENCES

Strips of wind
tie night
around
Newfoundland.
Two very young girls,
their hands evening red,
giggle themselves off balance.
A man asks them the time.
They run.

YOU COULDN'T WAIT FOR SPRING

for Lee-lee

The birthday card you sent
two weeks early said,
we were pals.
I liked the part where
your name was signed slow.
Once, I turned your room around.
You noticed the bed when you went
for the dresser.
You made the steps sing.

Your home was somewhere.
I only know that.
Three floors made your soft knees
buckle.
Now,
you sleep like an unsigned card.
Sent from one pal
to another.

SIMPLE

for the folks at the
West 43rd St. Nursing Home

This is where old people are left
to get older.
It is their job,
like selling shoes.
This building has old on its face;
brown patches left to get browner.
I walk by to make sure
I am out here.
Not inside, counting corners.

Two people are in the courtyard.
From here,
it appears to be a son
visiting his mother.
The mother folds into a chair,
and breathes so I can hear.
I see her only
from behind,
like a building cold in its own shadow.

Past them now,
I look back.
Oh God,
nothing so simple as this.
No mother in that chair,
but a young boy.
He cannot lift
or suck in.
His father feeds him with fingers
that wipe his cheek.

I look for any place
to shrivel,
like fruit left too long
on the counter.
At the West 43rd St. Nursing Home,
there is no place
to hide.

NOT BELIEVING THERE REALLY IS
A ROCKPORT, CALIFORNIA

A town can get lost.
The fishermen might all move
North,
netting lumberjacks with them.

Rockport is on no one's map.
Not a high school football schedule
or a library
with door handles that stick.

A man in Fort Bragg says, something is there.
He can't remember.
Thelma said, in Westport,
"Here, take this chicken.
You might get hungry on the way."

All of this to go on.
Night came like
an appetite. We settled still
hungry
to be one town over.

THE NICE PEOPLE WHO JUST
WANTED YOU TO KNOW

There are more nice people.
They go to airports and hope planes land safely.
They offer you their seats.
In the olden days,
nice people stayed inside.
There, they could count their blessings.
Those nice people knew each other's
middle names.
Nice people have nice middle names.
They wait to eat their soup
and do not sip.
A nice person remembers to wear a watch
and looks at it on the hour.
No nice people ever forget
to bleach their underwear.
If all the nice people in the world
piled into a phone booth,
it would topple, nicely.
When a nice person meets another
nice person, they both get nicer.
They say two nice people
could start their own religion,
or television game show.
There are enough nice people to sew on
all our missing buttons.
The nice people you know
are trying to tell you something
When you die,
they will all send
nice cards.

STAY

For Eag

What is this thing
inside
your lungs?
Cancer cells are growing
like mushrooms no one planted.
I want to run them over
with a lawn mower;
dig their roots out with a hoe.
I would give you my lungs,
my blood.

I should have known
you knew.
When you didn't renew
our season tickets on the 50 yard line,
I believed your excuse
about too many losses
last year.

Stay.
I want you to stay
for me.
I want you to be my best man,
bounce my children
on your knee.
They can't grow up without feeling
your hands.
You would be the grandfather
who sings.